DATE			

The Sierra Club Wayfinding Book

The Sierra Club Wayfinding Book

Vicki McVey

Illustrated by Martha Weston

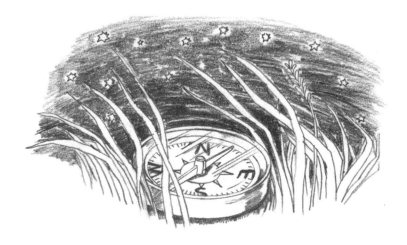

SIERRA CLUB BOOKS
San Francisco

LITTLE, BROWN and COMPANY
Boston • Toronto • London

The Sierra Club, founded in 1892 by John Muir, has devoted itself to the study and protection of the earth's scenic and ecological resources — mountains, wetlands, woodlands, wild shores and rivers, deserts and plains. The publishing program of the Sierra Club offers books to the public as a nonprofit educational service in the hope that they may enlarge the public's understanding of the Club's basic concerns. The Sierra Club has some sixty chapters in the United States and in Canada. For information about how you may participate in its programs to preserve wilderness and the quality of life, please address inquiries to Sierra Club, 730 Polk Street, San Francisco, CA 94109.

Text copyright © 1989 by Vicki McVey
Illustrations copyright © 1989 by Martha Weston

First Edition
All maps by Vicki McVey

Library of Congress Cataloging-in-Publication Data

McVey, Vicki.
    The Sierra Club wayfinding book / by Vicki McVey; illustrated by Martha Weston, [all maps by Vicki McVey]. — 1st ed.
       p.   cm.   R00765 26618
    Includes index.
    Summary: Describes how humans have developed systems using their senses, landmarks, maps, navigation, and signs in the natural world to find their way around. Includes activities, games, and experiments illustrating the principles of wayfinding.
    ISBN 0-316-56340-4
    1. Orientation — Juvenile literature.   [1. Orientation.]
I. Weston, Martha, ill.   II. Title.
GV200.4.M48 1988
796.5 — dc19   88–11124
                                                                    CIP
                                                                    AC

Sierra Club Books/Little, Brown children's books are published by Little, Brown and Company (Inc.) in association with Sierra Club Books.

10 9 8 7 6 5 4 3 2 1
BP

Published simultaneously in Canada by
Little, Brown and Company (Canada) Limited

PRINTED IN THE UNITED STATES OF AMERICA

For the children

Contents

...or How to Find Your Way in This Book.

1

Getting Lost and Finding the Way

What is a "way"? If you don't know where you are, it is something you have lost. If you don't know where you are going, it is something you are looking for. And if you do know, it is something you can show someone else. One of the most ancient skills that we possess is the ability to find our way from one place to another: *wayfinding*.

People who have been lost once don't want it to happen again, so they learn how to keep track of where they are. They do things like counting stars, marking trees, memorizing turnings, and drawing maps. But no matter what people do to keep from getting lost, all of their methods have one thing in common: they have been used before. It has been many thousands of years since we humans learned how to move around in our environment. Our primitive ancestors devised ways of figuring out where they were and how to get where they wanted to go, and we have been using and improving on their methods ever since.

Most of us consider — and we are usually right — that we can move safely from one place to another. But part of the reason most of our journeys are safe is that we know where we are at any given moment

and how to get where we are going. If we lack that information we are lost, and we are no longer absolutely safe. Here is an example of what it is like to be lost:

Jesse had lived for a few years in the Coast Range Mountains of northern California. One rainy afternoon he was trying to find a shortcut home through the woods. Sloshing through the trees with his wet dog, he expected to come at any moment to the huge, crooked ponderosa pine that marked the clearing around his cabin. This was a special tree to Jesse, not just because he loved its strange shape, but because it was a landmark, which he could see from any direction, that meant he was almost home.

This time, though, he had walked for several miles and still there was no tree; or, rather, there were thousands and thousands of trees, but not *his* tree. He turned all the way around two or three times, searching through the forested slopes for that one particular ponderosa pine, feeling smaller and smaller as it failed to appear. When he finally stopped turning he knew that he was just one small person in the middle of a huge forest and he was lost.

It was late afternoon and Jesse and his dog had been walking since late morning: several hours into town and several more returning. It had been raining all day, and he felt as wet and slick inside his poncho as the frogs that lived in the stream by his cabin. He wandered first in one direction and then in another, hoping to find the stream so he could follow it up to the clearing.

Finally he heard running water, but when he got closer he discovered that it was flowing the wrong way. Since he knew that streams don't change their directions, Jesse decided it was time to sit down on the nearest stump to do some serious worrying.

He applied himself so diligently to the task that it took him longer than it should have to notice that his dog wasn't paying much attention to their serious plight. In fact, she didn't even seem to realize they were lost. As he watched her nose her way around the trees, looking for small things to chase, it finally occurred to Jesse that, in fact, the dog *wasn't* lost.

It was almost dark, and neither Jesse nor anyone else knew where he was. It seemed to him that things were about as bad as they could get, so he decided to gamble on the dog. "Go home!" he ordered, and when she shot off, he followed her. He knew all about wandering because that's what he had been doing for the last few hours, so he could tell right away that his dog wasn't wandering.

She moved without any hesitation in and out of the same trees they had been stumbling through minutes before, and after half an hour or so Jesse finally saw his crooked ponderosa pine. He felt tremendous relief, but he also felt very foolish. He had lived and walked in those hills for several years; how had he gotten lost?

Webster's *New World Dictionary of the American Language* (Second College Edition) says that lost means "having wandered from the way; uncertain as to one's location." According to Webster's, then, in order to be lost you must first have been on a "way." We have lots of expressions that use that word, such as "He's on his way home," "I know my way to the library," and "It's on the way to the airport." It is interesting to notice that some "ways" belong to the person who is following them (*his* way home, *my* way to the library), and some are public ways that belong to everyone (*the* way to the airport).

If you are following a public way, there are at least two reasons why you shouldn't get lost. First, there are probably signs to direct you, and second, there are usually other people around to ask for help. But what about the private kind of way, the kind that belongs to the person who is following it? If you wander from that, then you have really lost your way. Private ways exist in the minds of the people who walk on them. For instance, nobody knows my way to Alfalfa's market unless I tell them what it is. And then, if they use it, it becomes their way, too.

Like every one of us, you carry around a huge atlas of private-way maps in your head. For every place that you have learned to go — especially if you figured it out for yourself — there is a "mental map" tucked away somewhere in your memory. Sometimes these mental maps are transferred to another surface. For instance, if your friend asks you the way to your house, you might transfer your mental map to the back of an old envelope and give it to him. People draw maps on all sorts of things — sand at the beach, dust on the trunk of a car, paper napkins, and even their hands. But whether you share your own mental maps with anyone else or not, you use them every day to get from one place to another.

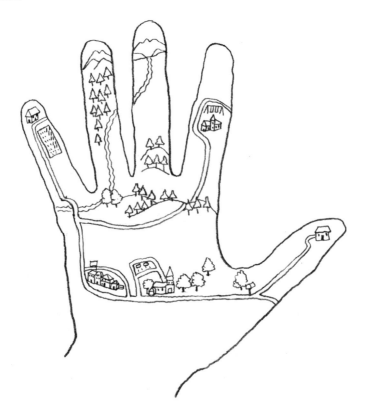

We talked about signs or markings on public ways (for example, "INTERNATIONAL AIRPORT NEXT LEFT"), but private ways have signs, too. What kinds of signs do we look for along our various ways? When I was very small there was a particular chain-link fence with a snarling beast behind it that I avoided by going through an alley. That fence marked the way I *didn't* want to go. Or how about Jesse's crooked ponderosa pine? That tree was the sign that marked the end of his way home, and Jesse's story illustrates just how important such "waysigns" can be.

So far we have been talking about signs that we can see (landmarks), but our other senses can also give us clues about our location. Have you ever known anyone who lived near a bakery? Follow your nose to his or her neighborhood. Or an airport? Follow your ears. A rushing river can often be heard, smelled, and even felt long before it can be seen.

In many types of environments, especially those referred to as "featureless," there are very few visual clues to help the people who live in them find their way. These places are usually quite flat, have little or very scrubby vegetation, and almost no other visible landmarks. Such environments include the desert, the Arctic tundra, the savannah, and the ocean.

People who live in or near these places develop especially keen senses for detecting minor changes in the landscape. As you might guess, they tend to be particularly skilled wayfinders and their lives often depend on their ability to recognize and decipher nonvisual messages from the world around them.

It is clear, then, that signs and other clues from the environment keep us on our way, and if we get lost, it is often because we can't find or recognize these clues.

The other part of Webster's definition of lost was to be "uncertain as to one's location." If we substitute "completely confused" for "uncertain," the definition might be more accurate, but otherwise it is a good one. When you know where you are, you know your location, and when you are lost, you don't. But how do you know your location? In addition to signs and clues from the environment, you need to know three things: your position, direction, and distance from another known place. In Chapter 2 you will learn about these three components of location, and by the end of the chapter you will begin putting your new knowledge to use.

Because this book is going to take you on some wayfinding journeys of your own, you will need something that the explorers of our world have used for centuries: a journal. This will help you keep track of the sights, sounds, smells, and sensations of the world you are going to explore. A small notebook makes a handy journal.

Some of your journeys, explorations, and activities will involve a partner, so if there is a friend or member of your family that you especially like to do things with, you might invite her or him to go through this book with you.

2

How Do We Know Where We Are?

The first component of location is *position*. Although we all understand the position of the earth as a planet that orbits around the sun, not too many hundreds of years ago people were still ignorant of the true position of the earth, believing our planet to be the center of the universe with everything else in orbit around us. Position is one of those things that can only be known in relationship to something else; in other words, it is relative. We now know what the earth's position is relative to the sun.

An experience my friend Erica had illustrates the importance of knowing your true position. She had an appointment in a building in which each side of the modern, rectangular lobby was like a mirror image of the opposite wall. On each end of the lobby there were glass double doors leading to the outside, and the other two walls, forming the long sides of the rectangle, were identically composed of elevator doors and large ashtrays with nondescript paintings hanging above them. When Erica arrived for her appointment she parked her bike in the racks outside the entrance, went into the building, and took the elevator to the third floor.

Half an hour later, when she had completed her business, Erica rode back down on the elevator, went out the big glass doors, and walked over to the bike rack. But the bike rack wasn't there. She automatically turned her head to where she expected to see mountains in the distance, and felt a moment of panic when she realized that they weren't there either. When she had walked into the building just half an hour before, she had passed through a concrete courtyard surrounded by bike racks and benches. Now there was a big lawn edged by sidewalks and buildings.

After a few dizzy moments she realized what had happened. She walked back into the building, and then left again, this time through the correct door. The mountains were back where they should have been, her bike was in the rack on the edge of the courtyard, and her mind was once again in synch with reality.

When Erica had stepped out of the elevator in the lobby she had turned the wrong way and left the building on the opposite side. She had been confused about her position relative to the outside doors.

The other two components of location are direction and distance. *Direction* is a word we use almost every day without even thinking about it, as in "I'll give you directions to my house" or "Which direction is the rug market from here?" or "Follow directions."

"Well, which direction *is* the rug market from here?" I asked the taxi driver. I was in a small town in the mountains of southern Mexico, and it was so foggy and rainy that I couldn't see very far in any direction. "Toward the mountains," he said. "Thank you, but which direction are the mountains?" I asked. "Oh, to the west," he replied. Feeling slightly stupid, I asked him which way was west. He scratched his head, pointed over his shoulder to a glow in the clouds just above the horizon, and explained to me as if I were his very small daughter, "West is where the sun is setting." "Ahh, *muchisimas gracias,*" I said, and turned west to look for the rug market.

North, south, east, and west are natural directions determined by the spin of the earth on its axis as it revolves around the sun. East and west are pretty easy to figure out because the sun comes up, crosses the sky, and goes down in the same direction every day. So, anywhere on the planet, east is the direction where the sun rises, and west is the direction where it sets.

North and south are slightly more complicated. A simple way for determining north and south, provided that it is night and the sky is free of clouds, is to look for the star or stars that are most directly above the North or South Poles. Those are Polaris (or the North Star) in the Northern Hemisphere, and the Southern Cross in the Southern Hemisphere.

Long ago the Chinese developed a more complicated but also more reliable method for finding north-south directions. It happens that lines of magnetic force from inside our planet move out into space at the approximate locations of the North and South Poles. The ancient Chinese were the first to realize that a magnetized piece of metal would always line itself up with these points of magnetic concentration. They used a free-swinging magnetized needle as a pointer. That was sixteen hundred years ago, and we are still using the magnetic compass today.

Although most people throughout the world recognize and use what we call the *cardinal directions* — north, south, east, and west — other cultural groups have developed unique systems of reference for direction. Some of these systems are very simple, and others are extremely complex.

Two groups that use only two directions are the Yurok Indians of northern California, and the Tikopians, who live on a small island in Polynesia. The Yurok are fishing people. They get almost all of their food from the Klamath River, which flows right through the middle of their land. They also depend on the river for transportation: if they need to go someplace, the river takes them. But since they spend all their time either on the river or next to it, they only need to go two directions: *upstream* or *downstream.*

Like the Yurok, the Tikopians live in a fairly small area. Their world is an island that is small enough that, wherever they go, they are still within sight, sound, or smell of the ocean. You might guess that their two directions are *inland* and *seaward.* An anthropologist who spent some time on Tikopia once overheard one islander say to another, "There is a spot of mud on your seaward cheek."

A much more complicated system of directions is one used by the Chukchee of Siberia, in the northern Soviet Union. Their compass identifies twenty-two directions and is three-dimensional. Our system is flat: no matter whether you are going north, south, east, or west, you will just be traveling back and forth. But Chukchee directions go back and forth, *and* up and down.

The third and last component of location is *distance*. As with position, distance is relative. We must know how far we are from some *other* known point in order to accurately locate ourselves. Most cultures think of distance as separation not only in space ("My house is four miles from the center of town"), but also in time ("The hotel is only ten minutes from the airport").

Many American-Indian groups measured distance by counting the number of suns or full moons it would take to travel from one place to another. This was a very practical way to consider distance. If you knew that you lived three days from the next village, you would also know how much food to carry with you.

The BaMbuti Pygmies of the Congo rain forest are an example of a group that has no cultural concept of distance. Because their entire

world lies within a thick forest, everything they see is viewed from close up. Outside of their own environment they are very confused by objects that are visible across the distance.

Colin Turnbull, an anthropologist who worked with the BaMbuti, once traveled with one of the forest people named Kenge to an area of open grassland outside of the rain forest. Looking down across the flat land, Kenge saw some buffalo from a distance of a few miles away. He turned to Turnbull and asked what kind of insects they were. When the anthropologist replied that they were buffalo, Kenge burst out laughing and told him not to tell such stupid lies.

Not ever having seen into the distance before, Kenge was unaware of the concept of perspective and could not judge how big the buffalo were, nor how far he was from them. If he had needed to travel out across the grassland he would have gone with neither the food nor the water to complete the journey.

How good are you at judging distance? In the following games and activities you will put some of the information about position, direction, and distance to use. After you have experimented with each of the components of location, you will play a game that puts them all together.

—————— Mom's Closet Game ——————
(Position)

This game you can play by yourself. All you need is a completely dark closet (you'll probably have to wait until nighttime) and an ability to concentrate. If you can't find a closet big enough to turn around in without touching anything, try the bathroom.

Go in the closet, close the door, and turn so you are facing it. The room must be absolutely pitch-black — no light showing under the door! Close your eyes and concentrate on your position relative to the door. With your eyes still closed, turn around five times, trying to keep track of your position. Stop at the end of the fifth turn when you think you are once again facing the door, and step forward until you touch something. Is it the door?

Making a Compass
(Direction)

Two of these compasses are magnetic, and two use sun and shadow. You can decide for yourself how many you want to make, but I suggest that you make at least one of each kind. (These compasses give only a general indication of direction, which is perfect for our purposes, but not accurate enough for real navigation.)

The first two compasses involve magnetizing a needle. You will need a needle and some kind of fairly strong magnet (most strong refrigerator magnets will do). Attach one end of the needle to the magnet, and leave it overnight. The next morning you can test the needle by using it to pick up another needle or small pin.

FLOATING COMPASS. For the floating compass you will need a cup of water and a small piece of cork. Put the magnetized needle through the piece of cork so it is balanced roughly in the middle, and then carefully float the cork in the water. Carry the cup through the house, outside, anyplace you want to go, and see if it always stays pointed in the same direction.

SWINGING COMPASS. The swinging compass is even simpler. Just tie a long thread around the middle of the needle, and let it hang. Move the thread back and forth on the needle until you find its center of gravity and the needle hangs parallel to the ground. The needle will turn and swing until the kinks are out of the thread, and then it will stay pointed in the same direction no matter which way you move.

One odd thing about these two compasses is that although in each instance the needle aligns itself in a north-south direction, you don't know which is which. That's one of the peculiarities of electromagnetic energy: no matter how you put the needle on the magnet, you don't know which end will be attracted to the north and which to the south.

To find out which end of the needle points north, take the compass outside. Stretch your arms straight out, and turn your body so your arms are pointing north-south, like the magnetized needle. If it's before

noon and the sun is in front of you, your left hand is pointing north. (You can figure out the other possible combinations for yourself.) Once you know which way north is, you can identify it with either the pointy end of the needle or the end with the eye.

MAJOR MIKE'S SHADOW STICK. Find a straight stick a little more than one foot long, and push it into the ground so that about a foot of it is exposed and pointing straight up. Try to bury it in a place that will be in the sunlight for several hours.

When you first put the stick in the ground, find a small rock and place it exactly on the end of the shadow of the stick. Wait about an hour to give the shadow a chance to move, and then go back and put another small rock at the end of where the shadow is now resting.

Now, put the tip of your left foot on the first rock, and put the tip of your right foot on the second rock. Your body will be facing exactly north.

WATCH DIAL COMPASS. A digital watch won't work for this compass, so you'll need one with hands. (If it is summer and you are on daylight saving time, set the watch back one hour.) Holding the watch flat, turn it so the hour hand (the short one) is pointed directly toward the sun. Halfway between this point and the twelve o'clock position on your watch is south.

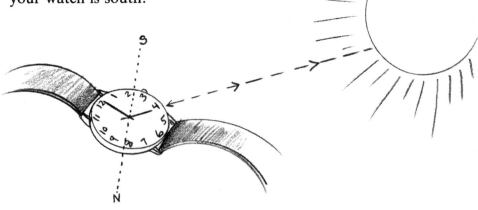

Pacing Game
(Distance)

Your footsteps can be counted as a way of measuring distance, but first you must determine the length of your own "pace." To do this all you need is someplace to walk and a tape measure.

Pull out the tape measure and lay it in a straight line along the ground. Go back to the beginning of the tape and walk along it at your natural pace, counting each of your footsteps. When you reach the end of the tape, divide the number of inches you have walked by the number of steps you have taken, so you'll know how many inches long your pace is. (Mine is about 31 inches.) There are 63,360 inches in a mile; divide that by the number of inches in your pace to find out how many of your paces there are in a mile. (A person with a pace of 31 inches will walk about 2,044 paces in a mile, or about 511 paces in a quarter of a mile.)

After you have figured out what your pace is, make a list in your journal of some of the places that you walk to. Make a guess at how far each place is from your house, and write it in parentheses next to the place: for example, "Abe's house (½ mile)." Then take your journal and your pencil, put some pebbles in your right pocket, and go find out how accurate your guesses are. As you walk, count only your right footsteps. Every time you count to one hundred, take one of the pebbles from your right pocket and put it in your left. Because you're only counting half of your steps, each pebble will mean you have walked two hundred paces.

When you reach your destination, multiply the number of paces you've taken by the length of your pace. The sum is the total distance. (Remember: there are 63,360 inches in a mile.) Are the places closer or farther from your house than you thought?

Location Game

You'll need a partner for this game. One of you will bury a treasure, and the other will find it. The one who is going to bury it must decide on a location that is within sight of a visible landmark both of you can identify. The location can be either inside or out, but if it is inside, or if it is cloudy or dark outside, you'll find that the two sun-and-shadow compasses won't work.

If you are the one who is hiding the treasure, you must give clear, written instructions (not a map) stating the position, direction, and distance of the treasure from the visible landmark. You might come up with something like: "The treasure is downhill from the huge blue spruce, and one hundred yards northwest of it."

Because neither the homemade compass nor the pacing measure of distance will be perfectly accurate, you might need to give your partner some extra help, like: "Look for three rocks that form a triangle," or "It's near a bush with red berries," or some other good hint. After your partner finds your treasure, change roles and you become the treasure seeker next time.

The treasure is uphill by the fence and 50 yards south of something gross

3

Gathering Information for Wayfinding

The task of moving around in our world, of getting from one place to another, is so automatic that we rarely even think about it. We go to school, to the store, or to a friend's house. We walk, take a bus, ride a bike, or go in a car. But getting around, like any other task, is easy only because we already know how to do it. What does that mean, to know how to do something? To begin with, it means having information.

Imagine a machine. It moves over the face of the earth gathering information. Its entire surface is covered with tiny sensors for detecting changes in the temperature, humidity, and movement of the air around it, and for sensing vibrations in the earth underneath. At the end of its two upper extendors are small probes that are so sensitive they can trace a groove one twenty-five-hundredth of an inch deep in a smooth pane of glass and can grasp and manipulate tiny objects with wonderful precision.

Near the top of the machine are two dish-shaped devices for picking up sound waves and for sensing gravity and motion. There is also a complex mechanism that emits vibrations coded as language. Inside this mechanism is a system of receptors that can detect the presence of minerals, sugars, and acids, and just above it another device for sensing odors. Its most delicate sensing devices are for receiving light waves and translating them into clear, three-dimensional, moving colored images.

The information picked up by these various sensors is sent to the storage and processing unit of the machine. This unit processes the data sent into it and issues commands according to the new information it receives. In this way it is self-regulating. It can correct its own mistakes, analyze its environment, and move purposefully from one place to another, picking up new information along the way.

Have you guessed what kind of a machine this is? Would you like to have one? If you would, I've got good news for you. You're it! You are an amazing and wonderful organism that constantly gathers and processes information about the world around you. You use your senses of sight, hearing, touch, smell, and taste to collect information about your environment, and then you use your brain to understand the information and to make predictions and decisions. Becoming a skilled wayfinder means learning how to pay attention to and make use of all of your senses.

No other living creature "senses" the world the way we do. The bullfighter's bright red cape, waved to tantalize and enrage the charging bull, really tantalizes only the people in the audience. As far as the bull is concerned, the cape might as well be gray. In fact, to the bull and most other animals, it *is* gray, and so is everything else.

Humans are among the few creatures able to see in color. We also see in greater detail and in more depth than most other animals. And we see the world as a collection of separate objects, rather than just as a series of patterns, which is how most other animals see it.

Our sense of touch, too, is very special. Not only do we have hands like the finest of precision tools, but the nerves that give us "tactile" information are concentrated in our hands so that we can touch and feel the things we are handling. Only people and some monkeys and apes can do that.

Pigs feel with their snouts and mice feel with their whiskers, but pigs and mice can't pick things up with their noses or their whiskers. They can't hold something up to their eyes for a better view while they

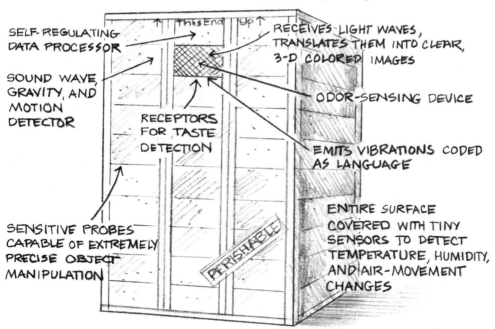

SELF-REGULATING DATA PROCESSOR

SOUND WAVE, GRAVITY, AND MOTION DETECTOR

RECEPTORS FOR TASTE DETECTION

SENSITIVE PROBES CAPABLE OF EXTREMELY PRECISE OBJECT MANIPULATION

This End Up

RECEIVES LIGHT WAVES, TRANSLATES THEM INTO CLEAR, 3-D COLORED IMAGES

ODOR-SENSING DEVICE

EMITS VIBRATIONS CODED AS LANGUAGE

ENTIRE SURFACE COVERED WITH TINY SENSORS TO DETECT TEMPERATURE, HUMIDITY, AND AIR-MOVEMENT CHANGES

PERISHABLE

touch it to find out what it "feels" like. In fact, because their eyes are so close to their noses or whiskers, they can't both feel and focus their eyes on an object at the same time.

Most animals have an advantage over us humans when it comes to smelling, though. Dogs can smell at least a hundred times better than we can, and if you watch a dog you will see that it investigates the world with its nose. Animals who get all their food by hunting often depend on their noses to help them find it. On the other hand, animals that *are* food depend on their noses to help keep them safe from the animals that are hunting *them*. A rabbit "sniffs out danger," and inside its tiny nose it has one hundred million chemoreceptor cells to help it identify odors. We haven't depended on our noses like that for millions of years.

The same thing that happened to our noses happened to our ears. As we (or our primitive human ancestors) began to find more and more of our food growing on trees or in the ground, and we didn't have to follow it as it tried to creep away from us, our ears became less important to our survival. That doesn't mean we don't use our ears. Our hearing, like our vision, is of the utmost importance in wayfinding. Sound, like light, moves in waves that travel in straight lines, so our ears can help us find directions.

Our sense of taste is closely related to our sense of smell, as you may have noticed if you ever had a cold on Thanksgiving and couldn't taste the feast. Although it keeps us away from some poisons and attracts us to sugars, salts, and other nutrients, our sense of taste seems less important for survival than any of the other senses. It is also less useful in wayfinding.

When we put together the information that is gathered by all of our senses, we experience the world around us as only human beings can. Dogs live in a fuzzy black-and-white world that is full of odors and sounds we can't even detect. Many birds see one scene out of one eye and an entirely different scene out of the other. Rattlesnakes can "see" things according to how much heat they radiate, so at night these snakes move in a world full of glowing objects.

All animals, including humans, have developed their own special skills to help them survive in this world. These skills involve putting information to the best possible use. If we learn how to pay attention, how to notice the messages that our five senses are constantly sending us, not only can we find our way from place to place without being afraid of getting lost, but we will enjoy our journeys even more.

Now we know that in order to be wayfinders, *we* have to pay attention to our *environment*. There are two parts to that: the *we* part, and the *environment* part. We have been talking about how *we* gather information. Now let's find out about the *environment:* clues in nature that help us know where we are.

The wind, for instance, brings clues to all our senses. This is especially true, whether we are in the city or the country, when we know the direction of the *prevailing wind*. Just about anywhere on earth the wind usually blows from the same direction, and this wind provides us with many clues to its presence — for example, trees with more branches on one side than on the other, and patterns in the snow or the sand.

Birds and animals naturally build their nests in the most protected places, so the presence of more nests on one side of rocks, bushes, and trees than on the other is a clue about the direction of the wind. If you see these things and already know where the prevailing wind comes from, then you automatically know which direction is which.

The wind certainly tells our sense of touch something. If you try the "wind walk" at the end of this chapter, you'll find that you can use the feeling of the wind on your body to maintain a constant direction when you are walking blind. And how about smell? The smell of a wind blowing off the ocean can lead you to the shore. The smell of wood smoke on the wind in the wilderness can lead you to other people.

Does the wind provide clues for our ears? Have you ever heard sounds carried on the wind? We often use sounds for locating directions, and the wind can help us do that. And finally, there's taste. Taste carried on the wind? That's not as silly as it sounds. A friend told me about being lost in a blizzard in the Arctic, and using the taste of the salt on the wind to guide him to the shore.

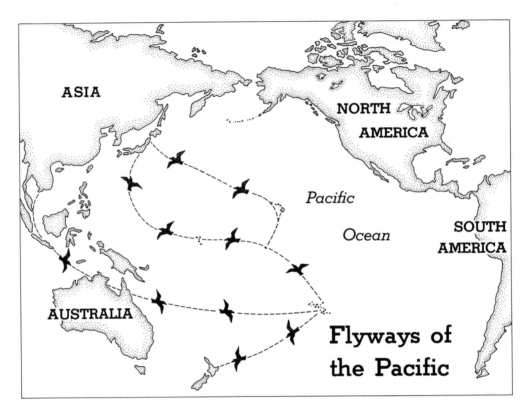

The sky is another source of natural wayfinding clues, but most sky clues are visual. Both the sun and the moon appear to travel from east to west, and can show us the cardinal directions. The stars have been our guides since people first started exploring our planet. The Caroline Islanders, some of the most famous navigators of all time, use star maps to travel throughout the islands of the Pacific Ocean.

Another natural clue in the sky is the path, or *flyway,* of migrating birds. The ancient Polynesians traveled thousands of miles from island to island using flyways to guide them. They also used clouds. In the Arctic and on the ocean, the underside of clouds acts like a mirror and reflects the presence of open water in the middle of ice, an iceberg in the ocean, or an island in the open ocean. An oasis in the desert is indicated from far away by the special haze it creates in the air above it.

Most of us are more likely to use the natural clues provided by various plants. In hilly areas, trees and bushes that grow on slopes facing north are different from those that grow on slopes facing south, and this difference in vegetation can tell you in which direction you're walking. Many plants orient themselves toward the sun, like the old man of the mountain, whose flowers face east. Other plants, like the compass plant, align their leaves in a north-south direction to provide themselves with shade. As with the prevailing wind, you have to get to know an area to learn how to read these natural clues.

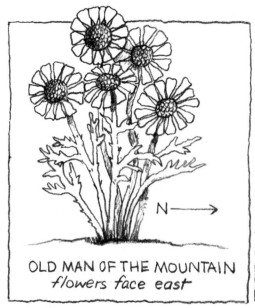

OLD MAN OF THE MOUNTAIN
flowers face east

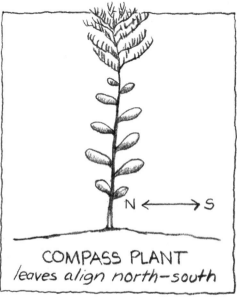

COMPASS PLANT
leaves align north-south

The environment provides us with information, our senses collect that information and send it to our brains, but what do our brains do with it? In the case of wayfinding, we store the information in "mental recordings" of the environment. Then, when necessary, we extract the appropriate bits of information and put them together as "mental maps." We are not even aware of this process.

Stop for a minute and think about how you get to your best friend's house, or to school. What did you do? If you're like most people you conjured up stored information: "Um . . . there's an ugly red house on the corner where I go left until I get to a noisy, busy street. That's the street before my friend's house, so I cross it, go one more block, turn right at the corner with the dog that always barks at me, and my friend's house is the third one on the left." That is a mental map. Did you notice that the "waysigns" ("ugly red house," "noisy, busy street," "corner with the dog") either indicate places to turn or confirm that the pathfinder is on the right course?

Like most mental maps, this one could be transferred to a scrap of paper and given to someone else who could then use it to get to the same place. Each person has her or his own absolutely unique mental maps, because each of us notices different things as we make our way from place to place. Of all the thousands and thousands of maps in the world, the most numerous and often used are the ones we carry around inside our heads.

Now we have a complete cycle: our five senses collect the information that the environment is presenting, and our brains process that information and make it available to us in the form of mental maps that help us get from place to place. The trick is that the more we notice, the more complete and accurate our mental maps will be. How good are you at noticing? Would you like to sharpen your wits and your senses? Here are some games and activities that will help you to do just that.

Observation Game

This game will teach you how to observe carefully, and to remember what you have seen. You can either play it by yourself or with a partner. Besides your journal and something to write with, you will need a watch that tells time in seconds and a place you aren't familiar with. The place may be a park, street corner, bus station, doctor's office, bank building, unfamiliar store . . . you choose.

You need to arrive at your chosen place without looking around to see what's there. If you are playing with someone else, your partner can lead you. If you are playing by yourself, you have to get there carefully and safely, but once there, look at your feet and don't raise your eyes until you are ready to begin the game. For exactly ten seconds, look quickly and carefully in every direction. At the end of the ten seconds, make a list in your journal of every single thing you remember seeing.

If you're playing with a partner, the person with the longest list wins the game. If you are playing by yourself, try to improve your score each time you do it. You'll find that you can play this in many boring situations, like while waiting for a dental appointment, or waiting for a bus, train, or plane. This game will vastly improve your powers of observation.

—————— Sun Walk/Wind Walk ——————

This game can be played alone or with others. All you need is a large, empty, open area, like a large yard, a deserted parking lot, a meadow, or a beach. Do not play this game where there is any traffic!

It is designed to help you pay attention to your sense of touch. You are going to try to walk a straight course without being able to see, but using the feeling of the sun or the wind on your face to keep yourself on course. If you use the wind, you must first check to be sure that it is blowing from one steady direction.

Begin in a place where you can walk straight for some distance without running into anything. It is best if you can turn so that the sun or wind is hitting your face. Close your eyes and allow yourself to sense exactly where on your face the sun or wind is striking (it might be your right cheek, for instance). Once the feeling on your face is very strong, begin walking, keeping your eyes closed and always keeping the feeling of the sun or the wind in exactly the same place. Walk as far as you can without opening your eyes.

Once you have stopped, turn around and check to see if you have walked in a straight line. The more you do this, the better you will trust your sense of touch and the longer you can go without opening your eyes.

An Indian Game

This is a hearing game, and it is best played with several people. The perfect location for this game is a forest, so it's great to play on picnics or camping trips. One person is "it." She closes her eyes and counts to twenty. While she is counting, everyone else hides behind a rock or a tree or whatever. After twenty counts, she opens her eyes and looks around for five counts. If she sees anyone she points to them and they are out.

After she closes her eyes again, everyone tries to sneak up on her at once without making a sound. If she hears someone she points to them, and if she is right and a person is there, that person is out. Each person tries to sneak up and touch her without being heard. Anyone who manages to touch her is safe, but the first person to be eliminated is "it" for the next game.

—— Mr. Feynman's Bloodhound ——

This game is named after Richard Feynman, the man who invented it. He realized that even though humans can't smell anywhere near as well as bloodhounds can, our sense of smell is much better than most people realize. You will need at least one other person, and eight or nine books. (It's important that these books haven't been touched by anyone for a while.)

Take the books off the shelf without touching them directly with your hands (use a pot holder, gloves, or piece of clothing), and arrange them in a row. Now, the person who is the bloodhound must leave the room. Another person picks up one of the books, opens it, and puts it back in the row with the other books.

The bloodhound comes back and smells each of the books, trying to choose the one that has been recently handled. Mr. Feynman says, "A book that's been standing there awhile has a dry, uninteresting kind of smell. But when a hand has touched it, there's a dampness and a smell that's very distinct."

4

How Other People Find Their Way

Of all the landscapes on earth, the most difficult for wayfinding are those with few or no visible landmarks: the ocean, the desert, and the polar regions. There are people in our world whose cultures have developed in such featureless environments, and it is among them that we can look for the greatest wayfinders.

The Pacific Ocean covers almost one third of the earth. It is a massive body of water 63,800,000 square miles in area, and there are people who live on tiny islands in the middle of it. They can't see anything from horizon to horizon except water, and yet they set out in canoes for other tiny islands, days and days away in other parts of the middle of the ocean, and get there. These are among the most amazing wayfinders of all time.

The art and science of navigation is taught in the central Caroline Islands as it has been for hundreds of years. On the island of Satawal, in the men's house, or *ut,* the chief of a family of navigators puts down a mat, and that is the signal for school to begin. When the mat was laid down almost a year ago, twelve-year-old Ikuliman, chosen by his clan to be a navigator, entered the world of his fathers and grandfathers.

You wouldn't recognize Ikuliman's school as one of the greatest on earth. There are no desks, books, papers, or pencils. The classroom is as likely to be outside in the sun or on the ocean as in the shelter of the men's house. A lesson might involve squatting over pebble constellations arranged in the sand, or learning an ancient star song, or rolling on the waves of the ocean to learn its patterns and messages.

Last night Ikuliman, his grandfather, Ponimar the navigator, and four other men from his island, returned from a twelve-day voyage to the island of Guam. It was Ikuliman's instructional voyage, and it had been made in his grandfather's twenty-six-foot outrigger canoe. At the beginning of the trip, Ponimar had taken careful back bearings: sitting in the middle of the canoe, he faced back toward the island they were leaving and determined how much the current was pushing them off their set course.

By day, Ikuliman and Ponimar sat on the bench in the middle of the canoe, and sometimes one or the other of them would lie down in the hollow of the hull, close his eyes, and let his body roll with the canoe until he could feel and hear the message of the ocean's swells. At night Ponimar would watch the sky and sing the star song for Guam. The song was a memory device, sung by the navigators in Ikuliman's family for more than a thousand years, and it was still leading them across the vast ocean.

The song was like a thread that had been unwound over the centuries, handed on by every father, picked up by each son, never dropped.

It was a map woven into a song. Anyone who knew the song could follow the directions from star to star, a clearly marked path over the waves of the ocean, and get to the tiny island at the end of the song. (In school Ikuliman was learning hundreds of such star songs.)

On the second day of their trip back from Guam, they ran into a storm. The wind was so strong they had to lower the sail, and the canoe was tossed all night on the roaring, crashing sea. The men and the boy had chanted through the night, waiting for the storm to die so Ponimar could judge how far they had drifted off course. The storm was more powerful than anything Ikuliman had ever imagined, and he had tried not to look as cold and frightened as he was. But even in the worst moments Ikuliman hadn't worried about getting lost. He knew that his grandfather would read the map of the sun, the stars, and the ocean, and get them safely home.

Now they were back on their own island. Ikuliman lay on his sleeping mat and let the memories of the journey become part of his growing store of knowledge and experience. He remembered feeling the roll of the ocean as he lay in the canoe's hull, tuning his body so that it would recognize the pattern of the swell. He remembered the bird that circled over the canoe at dusk, giving them the clear message that they were within twenty or thirty miles of their destination. He remembered the smell of the island that came to them far out to sea and guided them in.

He knew that these memories were only the beginning. They would

be added to throughout his life, providing him with information that would become part of his own system of navigation. Wayfinding in a world of tropical islands and blue ocean would be Ikuliman's life's work. Among a group of seagoing wayfinders, he was chosen to steer his people to their seemingly impossible destinations. His position as navigator was a great and special honor.

This is not always the case in societies of wayfinders. Among the Eskimos of the Arctic, for instance, wayfinding is no one person's special job, but is part of day-to-day survival in some of the severest weather conditions and bleakest landscapes on our planet.

The North Slope of Alaska ends at the edge of the Arctic Ocean. During the winter months, the boundary between land and sea is pushed many miles out into the ocean by the vast sheet of ice, called the Arctic pack, that forms over the water. Throughout the coldest months, the only animals that live on or under the pack ice are polar bears and seals, and for that time these two animals are the only sources of food for the Eskimos that live along the coast.

During his fifteenth winter Migalik was, for one long month, the only able hunter in his family. His father, Patik, had seriously injured his foot in an accident. His little brother, Nauruk, was still too young to hunt. So during the time of "the moon with no sun," Migalik was the only one in his family who could go out onto the pack to bring in seals.

He left home shortly after dawn one morning. He walked out onto the "landfast" ice and searched for seals all morning on this two-mile-wide shelf of quiet ice that was anchored in the shallows along the coast.

When he had used up all his luck on the quiet ice, he thought about going beyond this unmoving shelf to the far greater mass of ice that extended for miles out into the ocean, drifting in the wind and on the currents. The Arctic pack was a dangerous place to hunt because wind and currents could either force it out to sea or into collision with the quiet ice.

Migalik found a crack between the quiet ice and the pack, and he knelt down to test the direction of the current. He cut a piece of sealskin thong off his boot, chewed it until it was moist, and then dropped it into the crack. He watched it sink under the edge of the ice and then drift east toward the land. Good. The current was keeping the pack pushed up against the coast. If he was very careful he could hunt out on the pack.

This time of year the sun never rose above the horizon, and even at midday the light was low and dusky. Now he would have only a few hours to complete his hunt and get safely back to the landfast ice before full dark. He stepped onto the pack and began looking for a fresh breathing hole in the ice — a sure sign that a seal was still using it to come up for air.

Within an hour he knew his gamble had paid off. He sat quietly by a breathing hole, and when the seal's head appeared above it, Migalik was ready. Performing a routine he had practiced for years, he shot the seal, secured it to a line, and heaved it out of the water and onto the ice. Though he worked smoothly and efficiently, he was slightly distracted by a thought that kept trying to surface in his mind like the seal in the water. He knew he would have to take time to capture the thought just as he had the animal.

Migalik sat on the ice, cleared everything from his mind, and hunted for the sensation that had been bothering him. Suddenly he stood up and turned to face the wind. It was no longer blowing out of the west, which meant that the pack ice was no longer being forced up against the land. He threw his rifle and hunting bag over his back, slung the line attached to the seal around his chest, and began trotting toward the frozen land, pulling the dead animal over the ice behind him.

It was growing darker as he neared the lead, or open crack, between the landfast and the pack ice. Even in the heavy dusk Migalik noticed a greater darkening in the sky up ahead, and he knew this meant a stretch of open water reflected in the clouds above it. When he reached the edge of the pack ice he saw that it was indeed drifting out to sea. He ran along the edge of the pack, hoping to find a place narrow enough

to jump across. Within a few minutes he came to a band of water he thought he could span with a running jump.

He took off his rifle and hunting bag and threw them across the gap. Then he tied the line with the seal on it to his *unaag,* a long wooden shaft tipped with an iron point. He threw the *unaag* like a spear over to the other side and got ready to jump across himself. He stepped back several steps and then ran and leaped across the icy water. His feet landed at the edge of the quiet ice, and he knelt there for a few moments waiting for his heart to pump at its normal speed again.

By the time Migalik had pulled the seal across the widening gap of water and was ready to walk home, it was completely dark. The moon wouldn't rise for several more hours and there were clouds hiding the stars, so it was almost totally black outside. As Migalik walked, he knelt down every once in a while to feel the snowdrifts in his path. He could tell by their shape which direction to walk toward his village.

When he finally reached home he had a great hunting story to tell, which was almost as important as the fat seal he had towed back. He knew that it had been a combination of luck and training that had gotten him off the pack ice and safely home, and he was once again grateful for the knowledge of his people, which had shown him the way. Migalik, like everyone else in his village, was a wayfinder out of necessity.

There are many other groups of pathfinders that practice the art and science of wayfinding as a matter of day-to-day existence. Among them are the Bushmen of the Kalahari Desert, who live in the southern tip of Africa. For nine months of the year, they have no water at all and must make do with the liquid found in various melons and roots. The Bushmen live in small family groups, and each group gets its food by hunting and by gathering the edible plants that grow in its own territory.

They don't live permanently in any one place but roam throughout their territory seeking food and water. Wherever they stop to camp, they build tiny grass huts, called *scherms*. Sometimes they just scoop out hollows to sleep in, line them with soft grass, and put two arching sticks up to mark the place the door would be if they had built an entire *scherm*. All the members of each small group know every bit of their own territory, even though it might be as big as two hundred square miles in area.

Dikai, like all Bushmen babies, learned how to track almost as soon as she could crawl. She could pick her mother's footprints out from everyone else's, even in the dry dust and grass. By the time she could walk, she was known in her band as a fearless child. She would toddle by herself clear out of sight of the camp, and then find her own way back. Following tracks, reading the message in a bent blade of grass or a tiny indentation in the dirt, was a matter of life or death to her people, and even among these excellent trackers she was known as a keen observer.

One day, when Dikai was eleven, she went with her eight-year-old brother, Dabe, to find an edible plant called a *bi*. She had noticed this particular plant growing in the veld (grassland) when her band had passed through during the last rainy season. She knew no one else would have gotten it, because only her own group gathered plants in that area, and they hadn't been there for many months. Their camp was in a very slight hollow, and once Dikai and Dabe had gone over the gently sloping hill in front of them, the camp was hidden in the vast expanse of the plain.

It didn't occur to Dikai to worry about getting lost. Every bush, stone, and tree for many days' walking in every direction was almost as familiar to her as the grin on her brother's face. And, like Dabe's silly, crooked smile, each had its own message. Today, the dried grass they walked on soon told her that a large lioness had passed that way within the hour and was only a mile or two ahead of them, going in the same direction. The lioness was young and healthy, had killed and eaten recently, and was in no hurry to get where she was going. All of this Dikai knew from the tracks of the animal ahead of her.

The presence of the lioness didn't worry Dikai any more than the thought of getting lost. She had been around lions all her life and had even spoken to a few of them, and so far none of them had considered her to be food. In fact, the only food that mattered to any of them at the moment was Dikai's *bi,* and they all seemed to be heading for it. She and Dabe were only a mile from the place where it was growing, and they were still walking behind the lioness.

Even though there were no bushes or trees to mark the place, Dikai knew exactly where she would find the tiny dried stem that would show where to dig for the plant. But long before they got there, Dikai realized that in all of the vast expanse of plain, the lioness had decided to take a nap on top of her *bi.*

"Great Lion, Big Lion, you are resting on my dinner," she said respectfully when she and Dabe had approached within talking distance. "I know it is hot, and you have found a nice place for a nap, but you are on my *bi* and must find another place."

As Dikai and Dabe walked a little closer, the huge animal heeded Dikai's polite request, rose up out of the grass, and sauntered away. When they got to the lioness' napping place, Dikai pointed with her toe to a single blade of grass with a tiny stalk of vine wrapped around it. In the hundreds of miles of grassland, she knew exactly where this one grass blade was, and when she dug in the ground beneath it, she found the root of the *bi* she and her brother had come to collect.

Neither Dikai nor Dabe had to pay attention to the path on their way back to camp, they just followed the obvious trail of their own footsteps. The two children had a good story to tell around the fire after dinner that night, and everyone laughed and laughed at Dikai's conversation with the lioness.

All of the people in these stories used their training to help them find their way. Did you notice that they used many of their senses together to gain more accurate knowledge of the world around them? The following games and exercises will help you learn more about your own world.

—————— Star Game ——————

Go with another person to a comfortable place outside on a starry night. Scan the horizon and pick out a landmark that you want the other person to identify. Look straight up in the sky from your landmark to the clearest, brightest, or most obvious collection of stars. Now, describe for your companion that configuration of stars, and include what his or her eye will see in the sky as it travels down to the landmark.

It could be something like this: "Look for a shape like a hunter's bow made of four bright stars. Just below the bow is one very bright star by itself, and under that a little cluster of stars that looks like a 'T'." Your companion tries to locate the configuration of stars and identify the landmark on the horizon.

Tracking Game

This is actually two games: one is played inside and one outside. Either can be played alone or with a partner.

Tracking inside the house is very interesting, because most people leave signs of their presence in a room after they have left it. (How many times has one of your parents asked you to *please* pick up after yourself?) Go into an empty room in your house, check it out very thoroughly, and decide who was the last person to have been in the room. Is there an empty cup or glass, a book or magazine lying open, pillows rearranged on a chair or couch? There are many small and large signs that can identify the former occupant of the room as one or another member of your family. I'm sure you can discover each one's personal "track," even if that person is very neat and tidy.

The outside tracking game involves looking for and drawing pictures in your journal of as many kinds of tracks as you can find. Whether you live in town or in the country, there are tracks all around. Worms make tracks; bugs make tracks; people, squirrels, dogs, cats, and birds make tracks — just about everything that moves leaves behind some hint of its presence. Once you've drawn pictures of the tracks in your journal, find a book in the library that will help you identify them. If you play this game often, you will find that you have developed a habit of looking for and identifying tracks of all kinds.

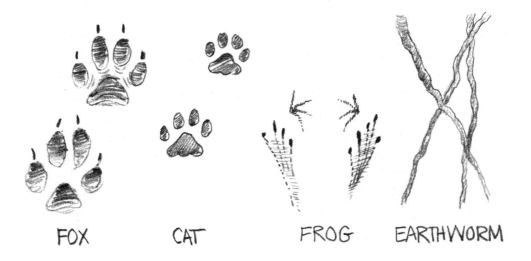

FOX   CAT   FROG   EARTHWORM

5

Coordinate Systems and Navigation

Have you ever heard the expression "**X** marks the spot"? As simple as it sounds, it captures one of the basic concepts of navigation: it is possible to locate any place on earth by identifying it as the point where two known lines cross. In navigation, each of those two lines is called a *line of position,* and the place where they intersect is a *fix.*

An **X** is two intersecting lines of position, but what would happen if you took an **X** apart? Well, you would end up with a \ and a /. As far as determining location is concerned, neither of those lines means anything by itself. It's like giving an address as "Broadway." You could walk down Broadway from its beginning to its end and never find the place you were looking for.

Broadway, in fact, is just one of the lines of position, and in order to get a fix, you need the other line. How about "the corner of 16th and Broadway"? That's good, because it gives you two intersecting lines: a street called Broadway and a street called 16th that crosses it. The system of naming and numbering streets, and giving each building an address that describes its location, is a type of *coordinate system.*

Coordinate systems are very important in the sciences of geography (including mapmaking) and navigation, which is really just a complex form of wayfinding. They help us understand how things are located on the surface of the earth. Did you ever think of your own address as a tool for navigation? If it has a number and a street name, that's what it is. Most city addresses are part of a *grid,* and a grid is part of a coordinate system.

As you can see in the illustration, a grid is made up of two sets of lines that all cross each other at the same angle. In this example, one set of lines is identified by letters, and the other by numbers. Suppose you want to find the point where the line marked "A" and the line marked "5" intersect. Put one finger on line "A" and another finger on line "5" and follow the two lines until they cross. That point of intersection has a kind of address that describes its location for anyone who wants to find it on the grid. Its address is "A-5." If you play the Galactic Mining Game at the end of this chapter, you will use the same sort of grid.

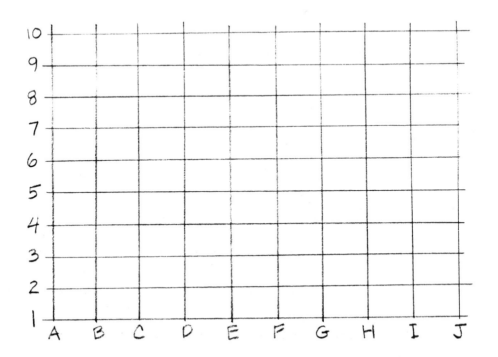

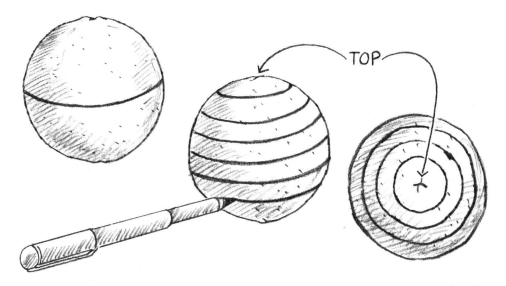

The best-known grid system in the world uses lines of *latitude* and *longitude* to create an address for any place on the earth. You might guess that drawing a set of grid lines on a round, or spherical, surface could create some interesting problems. If you would like to see why, you can try it yourself with an orange and a felt-tip pen.

First, hold the orange in one hand by its top (where the stem would be) and its bottom. Think of the top as the North Pole and the bottom as the South Pole. Now, draw a line right around the middle, as if it were a belt around a very round man. That line is the *equator,* because it divides the globe into two *equal* parts. It is also a line of latitude, and because it is right in the middle it has been given the number "0."

Since the earth is a sphere and forms a complete circle of 360 degrees, distances on it are measured in degrees. Each degree is broken down into 60 minutes (60′), and each minute is broken down into 60 seconds (60″), just like minutes of time. The equator is 0° latitude.

Now draw two or three lines around the orange above and below the equator, all parallel to each other. These new lines, like the equator, are lines of latitude, and they are also called *parallels*. They measure distance north and south of the equator. If you turn the orange so that you are looking down on either Pole, you will see that it looks like a target, with each parallel making a smaller circle inside a bigger one. The North or South Pole is the bull's-eye in the middle of the target.

Even though you have only drawn a few parallels on the orange, it is possible to make the lines so close together that they are almost touching. If you gave all these lines numbers, you could locate any place on earth as being so many degrees, minutes, and seconds north or south of the equator. The North Pole is 90° N, and the South Pole is 90° S. So from the South Pole to the equator is 90 degrees, and from the equator to the North Pole is 90 degrees. That makes 180 degrees, or half a circle. To get a complete circle of 360 degrees, count back down the other side of the globe: 90 degrees from the North Pole to the equator, and 90 more back down to the South Pole.

The town I live in happens to sit right smack on top of the fortieth parallel, so I know that I am exactly 40 degrees north of the equator (or 40° N latitude). But if I wanted to find my town on a globe, I wouldn't have enough information. I would know where to look up or down (north or south) from the equator, but the fortieth parallel runs all the way around the earth, and I wouldn't know whether to look east or west.

For that I need another set of lines. (Remember that a grid is made of *two* sets of intersecting lines.) To get the second set of lines, first draw a line from the North Pole of the orange to the South Pole. Then, draw one just like it on the opposite side so that it makes a complete circle all around the orange, crossing the equator on each side. These are lines of longitude that measure distance east and west. They are also called *meridians*.

Now draw several more meridians so the orange looks as it would if you peeled it and could see the sections inside. Once you've done that you almost have a complete grid system, but there is still something missing. How do you number the meridians? Which one is 0° longitude? The equator is the only circle that divides the globe in half from top to bottom, so it's easy to call it 0° latitude and number up and down from there. But what about the meridians? Any two of them together, if they are *exactly* opposite each other, divide the globe in half.

Back when the earth's grid system was first being numbered, many countries vied for the right to establish 0° longitude (or the *prime meridian*) in their own territory. Because there was no natural dividing line east and west, each nation claimed that the numbering system should start on its own land. Well, who do you think won? England. The prime meridian, or 0° longitude, passes through Greenwich (pronounced "Grennich"), England, and most countries measure distance east and west from there.

The meridian that is on the exact opposite side of the globe from 0° is 180°. But instead of being numbered from 180 clear up to 360, longitude lines go back down to 0° from 180° on the other side of the globe. That means that there are always two meridians with the same number, one west of the prime meridian and one east of it.

Now I can complete the address of my town so that I, or you, could find it on a globe. My town is located at 40° N latitude, 105°16′12″ W longitude. If you can find my town (or the city that's close to it) on a globe, then you have learned how to use a coordinate system.

The concepts of latitude and longitude have been used by sailors for thousands of years. Latitude is relatively simple to figure out. Anywhere on earth the sun reaches its highest point in the sky at noon, because that's when that part of the globe is directly facing the sun. But because of the earth's tilt, the position of the noon sun above the horizon changes as you move either direction away from the equator. A band around the middle of the earth, which goes from 0° to 23° north and 23° south, is the only area on the planet where the noon sun is ever directly overhead.

At the opposite ends of the earth, the North and South Poles (90° N and 90° S latitude), the sun never rises above the horizon in the winter season, and climbs only about 23 degrees into the sky at noon in the summer. At any latitude in between, by measuring the height of the noon sun above the horizon and keeping track of the time of year, you can know how far you are north or south of the equator. Latitude can also be determined at night by measuring the altitude of certain stars above the horizon, because that distance also changes as you move from the equator to the poles.

Figuring out longitude is a different story. There wasn't a simple, accurate way of determining longitude until the first portable, seagoing clock was invented in 1761. Do you wonder what time has to do with longitude? Well, the earth, like any other circle, is 360 degrees around its outside, or *circumference*. In one period of day and night, or 24 hours, it completes one full turn in relationship to the sun. If it turns 360 degrees in 24 hours, then it turns 15 degrees in one hour (or 360 divided by 24).

Now, we have already learned that the meridian that passes through Greenwich, England, is 0° longitude. That means that when it is twelve noon at Greenwich, its location on the planet is directly facing the sun. But what if you were 15 degrees west of Greenwich? The earth would have to spin one more hour to bring your particular spot into the noon position facing the sun, so it would only be 11:00 A.M. at 15° W longitude.

Let's put it another way. If you were on a boat in the Atlantic Ocean and you had one clock set for the correct local time and another clock set at Greenwich time, you could tell what your longitude was by the difference in the two times. If the boat clock said it was 11:00 A.M., and the Greenwich clock said it was twelve noon, you would know you were at 15° W longitude.

What happened during all those centuries before the invention of the seagoing clock? How did navigators determine their position in an east-west direction? Unfortunately, in the early years of navigation, it was pretty much hit and miss: either they hit the land they were aiming for or they missed it. Different people developed different methods for navigating, and, naturally, some were better than others.

The Vikings are an example of a group of people who learned to navigate well without being able to determine longitude. They *did* know how to determine latitude, however. They were great sea explorers (in fact, the Vikings visited North America several hundred years before

Columbus did), and they knew how to find a position north or south by "taking a fix" on, or "shooting," the sun. In other words, they used the elevation of the noon sun above the horizon to figure out how far north or south they should go. Of course, that meant that someone had to have visited a new land at least once to know how far the sun climbed above the horizon at that particular spot, at that particular time of year.

Sometimes the Vikings sailed to find a new land on the basis of a rumor. It is likely that the first Vikings to sail to Iceland based their journey on stories they had heard about Irish priests who found an island in the Atlantic Ocean. Following the rumor, the Vikings set sail in a longboat, headed north until the sun was at the right elevation at noon, and then turned left.

Of course, it was much more difficult and dangerous than that, but it's true that the Vikings sailed in a series of right-angle turns. They would head north or south until they got to the right latitude, and then turn either east or west. Although navigators today don't travel in right angles, they still use the sun and stars. This type of navigation, based on observation of the sun, stars, or other heavenly bodies, is called *celestial navigation.*

Pilotage is another class of navigation. It is a type of wayfinding that involves keeping track of location by following the progress of a journey on a chart or a map. Pilotage was used in the old days by seafarers who, instead of navigating the open ocean, followed shorelines and traced their courses on coastal maps. If you look at the map on the next page you will see that the Vikings used both celestial navigation and pilotage when they explored the oceans.

Pilotage is also used to navigate over land. Although most hikers don't know it, they are using this form of navigation when they take a cross-country hike using a map as a guide. We'll learn more about pilotage over land in the next chapter.

As you might guess, airplane pilots make use of this type of navigation. If you have ever flown, you know that unless there is a cloud cover between the plane and the ground, certain landforms, or *terrain features,* are highly visible from the air. In fact, many terrain features, like rivers, mountain ranges, and patterns of croplands, are easier to detect from the air than on the ground. Even airline pilots, who are in

Viking Navigation

GREENLAND

ICELAND

BRITISH ISLES

Atlantic

Ocean

EUROPE

Mediterranean Sea

Viking exploration

● ● ● Navigation by pilotage

---- Celestial navigation

almost constant contact with controllers on the ground, use pilotage to check their progress over certain features of the earth's landscape.

But like anyone else who is wayfinding, pilots sometimes get lost. During World War II there was a certain pilot named Vic, whose job was to teach other pilots how to navigate. He and the rest of his group lived in an Army Air Corps base at the head of the Brahmaputra Valley, in India. You can see the Brahmaputra River on the map on page 51. The arrow on the insert map *inside* the big map points to where the Brahmaputra River is in the world.

One time, when he was feeling particularly disgusted with army-style canned food, Vic got a terrible craving for an ice cream cone. That was quite a problem, because the nearest ice cream cone was half a day away by plane, in the huge city of Calcutta.

Well, Vic's craving finally got so disturbing that he decided on a day off to hitch a ride to Calcutta on a plane that was carrying mail. The pilots of the mail plane told him to make himself comfortable, so Vic settled himself on a sack full of letters in the back of the plane and went to sleep. He woke up a few hours later with the hot sun shining through a window in the plane onto his face. He lay on his mail sack for a minute, sensing that something was wrong, and then realized that the sun was shining in through the wrong side of the plane.

He went up to the cockpit and stood behind the pilots, who had a chart spread out between them and were trying to figure out where they were. He asked if they needed some help, and they were very eager to hear his suggestions. If you look on the map, you will see that the Brahmaputra River makes a right-angle turn before it heads south toward the Bay of Bengal and Calcutta. The simplest course would have been to cut from one end of the river to the other, forming a triangle. But the pilots had somehow gotten confused and were flying around in circles in the middle of the triangle, not sure which way to go.

They had been confused long enough that the plane was getting low on fuel, and there was a question about whether they should try to find Calcutta or look for the small airfield of the Maharaja of Koch Bihar. Vic knew that if they headed west they would eventually find the Brahmaputra River, and then they would have a line of position. When the plane crossed over the river, they could get a fix on their location by using pilotage to identify a particular feature of the river and find it on their chart.

So they headed west and, after a while, sighted the Brahmaputra. Vic found their location on the chart, and he discovered that they were, in fact, closer to the airfield of the Maharaja of Koch Bihar than to Calcutta. So the pilots landed the plane in Koch Bihar and borrowed some fuel from the Maharaja. After they had taken off again, they followed the river south and turned into Calcutta when they identified the correct location on their chart. Vic ate enough ice cream to satisfy

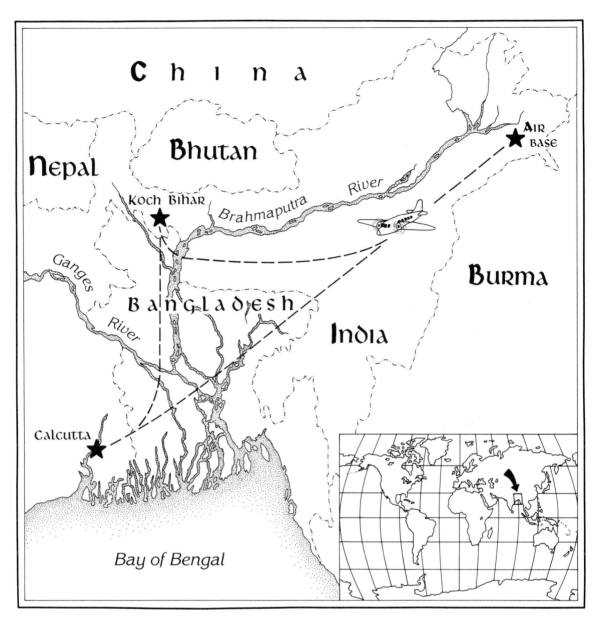

himself for another few months and then hitched back to his base at the headwaters of the Brahmaputra.

I like collecting stories about wayfinding, and this one is especially interesting to me because the pilot named Vic is my father. This story ended well because there was someone on the plane who knew how to navigate, and it illustrates for us how important such knowledge can be. Navigation is the actual science of wayfinding. Some forms of navigation use highly complex technology and require great skill and training. Other forms are simple and can be used by just about anyone.

In Chapter 2 you learned methods for estimating direction and distance, and now you know that you can determine your exact location by using two lines of position to get a fix. Grids provide the simplest way to establish lines of position, but you can also use celestial bodies for the same purpose. Here are some games and exercises that will sharpen your navigating skills.

Galactic Mining Game

This is a game for two people. Each of you will need to draw a grid like the one shown above. In this game there are two mining companies that mine asteroids in space for light metals. The names of the companies are the Black Hole Mining Company and Astro-Blast, Inc. You and your friend are prospectors, each one working for one of the companies.

Both companies are looking for metals on the same asteroid, and the procedure is that, using the grid, each prospector stakes five claims. To do this, you each circle five intersections on your own grid, every intersection representing one claim. Neither of you knows where the other person's claims are, but you must guess, using addresses like "A-5," "G-10," and so on. When you correctly guess the location of one of the other person's claims, that claim has been disputed and is no longer valid.

First, locate your claims on your own grid by circling five intersections (be sure that you can't see each other's grids). Now, taking turns, each one of you tries to dispute the other's claims by correctly guessing where they are. Each time you make a guess, mark that intersection on your own grid so you'll know not to guess it again. You can put a question mark on the wrong guesses and an *X* when you find one of the other person's claims. Each prospector gets one guess per turn. The first person to dispute all the other's claims wins the game.

Shooting Polaris

If you would like to know the latitude of your hometown, you can find out the easy way by looking on a globe or a map. But if you enjoy looking at the stars and would like to try something different, here's another way to determine latitude. People who practice celestial navigation use various heavenly bodies to find their position north or south of the equator. The simplest way of determining latitude, provided that it is night and the sky is clear, is to measure the altitude of the North Star (Polaris) above the horizon.

First, you have to find the North Star. Do you know where the constellation called the Big Dipper (or Ursa Major) is? If you don't, you can see what it looks like in the picture on page 55 and then find it in the sky. There are two stars in the Big Dipper, called "the pointers," that point to the North Star. Sometimes the Big Dipper is upside-down in the sky, so you have to remember to look toward the Little Dipper (also in the picture) instead of the other direction.

Here is how to determine your approximate latitude by the position of the North Star. If you stand up and point your arm straight above you, your hand is pointing to 90°. If you point straight out, you are pointing to 0°. Since 45 is half of 90, if you point midway between straight up and straight out, you are pointing to 45°. Now, on a clear night, go outside and find the North Star. Hold your arm out and point to it. If your arm were pointing straight up, you would be very close to the North Pole, or 90° N. If your arm were pointing straight out (and the North Star was on the horizon), you would be very close to the equator, or 0°.

You are probably going to be somewhere in between. My arm points to about 50° above the horizon, or a little more than halfway between straight up and straight out. To know what my latitude is, I subtract the estimated number of degrees of the North Star above the horizon (for me it's 50°) from 90°. According to this rough estimate, I live around 40° N latitude, and we know this is true because the fortieth parallel runs through my town. The hardest part of this exercise is estimating the altitude, between 0° and 90°, of the North Star above the horizon.

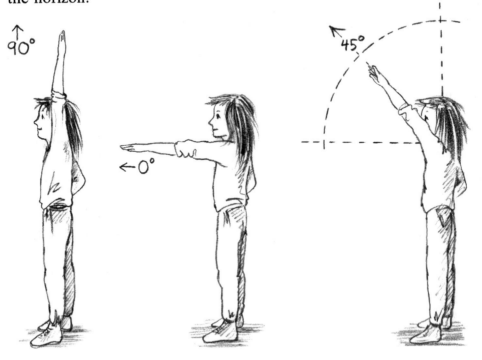

6

Maps and Wayfinding

There is a word that means "the art of making maps," and that word is *cartography*. Archaeologists think that our early human ancestors invented cartography before they invented writing, and that most cultures were making maps before they invented paper. It seems logical that our first efforts at written communication involved creating messages to help people to find their way. The earliest maps were probably made out of stone, and then later, of things like metal, cloth, and paper. Our words *map* and *chart* come from the Latin words *mappa,* which means cloth, and *charta,* which means paper.

The oldest map we know about is from Mesopotamia, an ancient civilization that developed in the area between the Tigris and the Euphrates rivers in what is now Iraq. This map is about 4,500 years old and is small enough to hold in the palm of your hand. It is made out of clay and has symbols scratched on it that represent things like mountains, towns, and rivers.

The earliest Greek map that has been found was printed on a coin made in the fourth century B.C. — or about 2,300 years ago. It is the first map we know of that shows *relief*, which is the elevation of different landforms, like mountains, above sea level. Another map from ancient times was drawn on the shield of a Roman soldier, showing the outlines of the Black Sea.

Although many maps made in ancient times were made out of things like stone, wood, and leather, not all maps made from natural objects are ancient. One of the most interesting and beautiful maps I've seen is made out of sticks, twine, and seashells. It is from the Marshall Islands, and it represents a type of map that was still being used there until fairly recently.

Do you remember the story in Chapter 4 about the boy, Ikuliman, from the Caroline Islands? Well, the Marshall Islands are "next door" to, but about a thousand miles away from, the Caroline Islands. The sticks on the Marshall Islands stick charts are made out of the middle part of a palm leaf, and they are tied together with string made from other plants. As you can see in the picture, small seashells, called cowries, are also tied to the sticks. The seashells are symbols that represent islands, and the sticks represent patterns of waves and swells around and between the islands.

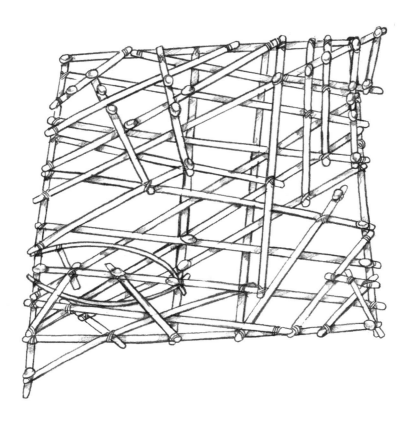

These maps, or charts, have been used by Marshall Island navigators for hundreds of years to locate islands that are too low in the water to be seen from a distance. A stick chart is accurate enough to lead people in small canoes, over an ocean that covers a third of our planet, to islands that can't be seen. That is a good map.

Since the invention of airplanes, and later of satellites, we have been able to take photographs of the ground from some distance up in the air. Cartographers can use these pictures, called *aerial photographs,* to draw very accurate maps. Many types of electronic devices are also used in mapmaking, and with greater technology and increasing knowledge of our planet, modern cartography has become a very advanced science.

One of the most important things to remember about the study of cartography is that it includes every sort of map you can imagine — and many that you can't. The high-tech maps of our own culture are only one class among the many types of maps that are made and used throughout the world. Their accuracy is created, tested, and proven with the help of sophisticated equipment used by highly skilled people. But maps made without the aid of electronic technology can be almost as accurate, and certainly as useful. The stick charts of the Marshall Islands are one example of this.

To give you another example, on the next page I have included three maps of Southampton Island in northern Canada, where the Aivilik Eskimos live. Two were drawn by the Aivilik. The third one was made from an aerial photograph. As you can see, they are very similar.

Southampton Island has over one thousand miles of coastline. It is easy for us to see the shape of that coast looking at the map, but from the ground it would be hard to determine. The eskimos who drew the maps had never seen their island from the air, but they knew every single one of those hundreds and hundreds of miles of coastline. The maps they drew from memory are "off" in a few places, but they are accurate and useful tools for wayfinding.

By now we have looked at and talked about many types of maps, and we know that a map isn't always something that is drawn or printed on paper. Printed maps are important, and we will spend some time talking about them, but don't forget about your own mental maps or

Southampton Island

Eskimo map

Eskimo map

Satellite map

some of the simpler maps drawn on the beaches, napkins, and dusty cars of this world.

What makes a map a map? Except for mental maps, all of the maps that we've talked about so far have some things in common. For one, all maps that are drawn or made are pictures that represent a particular location, space, or area. And they use symbols to describe that place.

A symbol is something that stands for something else, as **$** stands for dollars. On Long John Silver's treasure map, **X** marked the spot where the treasure was buried. On a map of Mexico that I have hanging on my wall, the color green stands for national forests, and little red tepees stand for campgrounds. Thick black lines stand for paved roads, and dashed lines are roads that are still being built.

The part of a map that tells us what the symbols mean is called the *legend,* or *key.* We usually use the word legend to mean some kind of story, and, in a way, a map legend is a story, too. It tells us what the map is all about. If you understand the legend, then you have the key to the meaning of the map. Next time you see a printed map (like the ones that are all folded up in the glove compartment of a car), take a look at its legend and find out what it's about.

Something else that all maps have in common is *scale*. If you have heard the term *scale model,* you probably know that is a small copy of a larger object, the way a dollhouse is a model of a house, and a model airplane is a model of a real plane.

A map is also a scale model. No matter how big it is, a map is smaller than the land area it represents. On many maps (especially those used for travel and navigation), you will find a message that tells you what the sizes and distances on the map mean. This is called the *scale*.

Scales can be shown in several ways. The one that is used most often is also the easiest one to read. It is called a *bar* or *graphic* scale, and it is a drawing that looks like a ruler. It shows how land area is measured on the map. On the bar scale shown below, one inch on the map is equal to five miles on the ground.

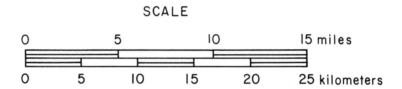

Here's an example of how to use this kind of scale. Let's say that you and your family are on a car-camping trip in Mexico, and you are driving down the Baja Peninsula on your way to Cabo San Lucas. By now you all know that gas stations can be few and far between, and that it's very important to watch the gas gauge on the car. Part of your job as chief map reader is to keep track of where you are and how far away that is from the next town.

You have been driving all morning, everyone is hungry, and the message from the gas gauge is that it's time to start looking for fuel. Your mom asks for a progress report; she wants to know how far you are from the next village large enough to have a gas station. You look on the map and see that you are about three inches from the next town.

You can't really say, "Well, Mom, we're only three inches from the nearest village," because, of course, it isn't true. You know from constant use of the map that one inch on the map equals five miles of real road, so you tell her that you are fifteen miles (or twenty-four kilometers) from the nearest gas station.

We have found three things that all maps (except mental ones) have in common. These are: (1) all maps are representations of a particular location; (2) they all use symbols to describe things at that location; and (3) they all use some sort of scale. Once you understand these things, you can read almost any map.

We learned in Chapter 5 that using a map or chart to keep track of the course of a journey is a form of navigation called pilotage. This kind of navigation over land is also called *orienteering*. There is one kind of map that is especially useful to the hiker who is practicing orienteering, and that is a *topographic* map. Topographic maps use special symbols to show the shape of the landforms, or *topography*.

If you are hiking in hilly or mountainous country, it is easier to find your way if you have a map that shows the shapes of the landforms. The symbols that are used to show this kind of topographic information are called *contour lines,* and here is how they work. Imagine that you put an ice cream cone (just the cone part — no ice cream) upside down on a table, and you wanted to draw a map of it, looking *straight* down, that would show its shape as a cone.

First, you could draw a line around the base of the cone where it was resting on the paper. (You would have a circle, wouldn't you?) Then, let's say that you measured all around the cone exactly one inch up from the table and cut the cone off along that line. If you put the cone back on the paper, so that it was in exactly the same position as before, it would fit inside the first circle. You could draw a line around the new base of the cone and it would be another circle, smaller than the first one. The new circle would represent all the points on the cone that were exactly one inch up from the table.

You could repeat the same process, each time measuring another inch up from the table, cutting another inch off of the cone, and then drawing around the new base. Each new circle would be smaller and would fit inside the last one. If you kept going up the cone in one-inch intervals, and drawing new circles each time, you'd end up with something that looked like a target, with the bull's-eye being the pointed end of the cone. Each one of the circles would be a contour line, and each contour line would include every point on the surface that was exactly the same elevation.

Now imagine that you could do the same thing with a mountain: measure and mark all the points, all the way around it, that were at the same height, or *elevation*. You could draw a line connecting the

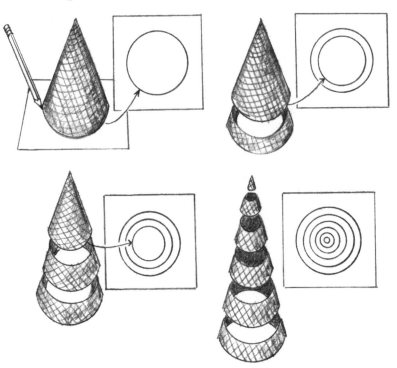

points, and then transfer that line (at a much smaller scale) to a piece of paper. The line on the paper wouldn't be a circle (unless the mountain were a conical volcano), but it might look something like the outline of a jellyfish, with a lot of curves and wiggles.

As you kept moving up the mountain, transferring lines onto the paper, you'd have smaller jellyfish outlines inside of larger ones. If this seems complicated and hard to understand, look at the section of a topographic map and the block diagram below. Here you can see the steps that turn a three-dimensional landform into a flat map.

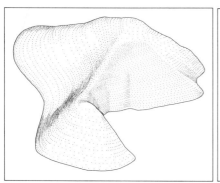 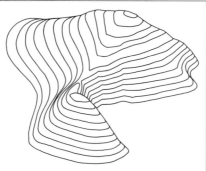 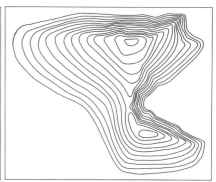

The most commonly used topographic maps in the United States are published by the U.S. Geological Survey (USGS). These maps give the person who knows how to read them a lot of valuable information. For instance, they tell the reader about the elevation of the land, or how high it is above sea level. If you were using the map, you would know whether you had to climb or descend to get where you wanted to go.

The map would give you this information in two ways. You could look for spot elevations, which identify the elevation of a particular point on the map (like a pass or a lake), and contour elevations, which give the elevation of an entire contour line. You can see on the map on page 64 that Arapaho Pass is 11,906 feet above sea level.

Another thing you can see, once you know how to look for it, is how steep the hill and mountain slopes are. On topographic maps, the closer together the contour lines are, the steeper the landforms. Where the contour lines are almost touching each other, the landform is like

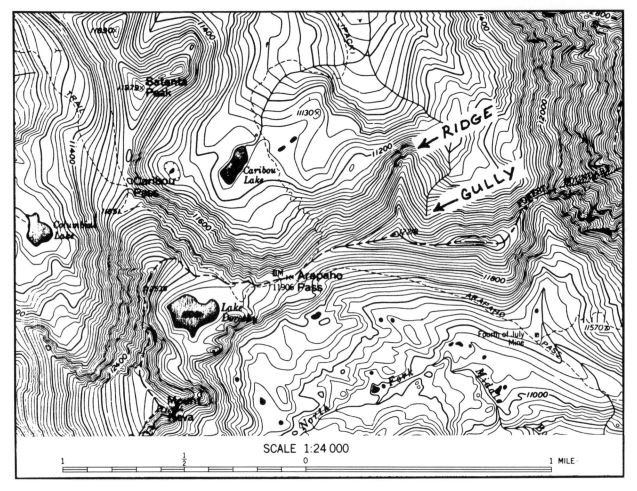

the face of a cliff. In places where the contour lines are farther apart, the land is flatter or gently rolling. In mountainous areas this may indicate a broad flat ridge, or a wide stream or river valley.

You can also see on the map that a series of V-shaped contour lines pointing toward the crest of the mountain indicates a stream or gully flowing down the side of it. V-shaped contour lines that point away from the top of the mountain indicate ridges. I have labeled these types of features on the map so you'll know how to recognize them.

Although the maps in this book are printed in black and white, on most USGS maps different colors stand for different features of the landscape. Contour lines and other natural landforms are printed in brown. Blue always stands for water (or ice). A solid blue line means a stream or river that flows year-round; a dotted and dashed blue line is a stream that flows only during certain seasons of the year. Blue contour lines are glaciers, and blue-colored areas are open water (lakes, oceans, and so on).

Black stands for man-made features like trails, roads, buildings, and towns. A dashed black line is a hiking trail (you can see several of those on the map). Parallel dashed black lines indicate dirt roads, and parallel solid black lines are what are called "light-duty" roads. Knowing how to read these symbols is very important to the hiker and backpacker. The map interpretation activity at the end of this chapter will help you learn to read "topo" maps.

Unless you are an experienced hiker, it is best to stay on a marked trail, but even if you always use trails it is sometimes necessary to rely on a map. It is never too soon to learn to read maps, so if you go hiking or backpacking with your parents or any other supervised group, try to get a copy of the topo map of the area you'll be hiking in. Fold the map so the section of trail you're on is to the outside, and put the map in a clear plastic bag to protect it. Keep track of your progress on the map.

Water features — rivers, streams, gullies, and lakes — are some of the best landmarks. Learn to notice those things and look for them on the map. They will help you know where you are, especially in forested areas where trees limit your long-distance vision. If you are walking above *tree line* (high elevations where trees are unable to grow) or in open areas, peaks and ridges are good landmarks. Learn to turn the map so that north on the map (usually the top of the map) is actually pointing north.

As you are hiking, turn around every once in a while and look back the way you have come. That way you can see what the trail will look like when you return. This is called *taking a back bearing,* and it should be done as a matter of habit. Another good habit is to constantly keep track of your position relative to a major landmark. As you walk around a ridge or peak, notice how it looks from every direction and remember what your path has been in relationship to it.

We learned in Chapter 3 that the greatest skill a wayfinder can develop is the ability to notice things. That is also true of orienteering, which is land navigation with the aid of a map and compass. When you are orienteering, not only will you be carefully observing the world around you, but you will relate your observations to the information on a map. The ability to read and interpret maps can be of the utmost importance, and it takes years of practice to develop. If you would like to start now, the following activities will get you on your way.

—— Making a Contour Model ——

The pattern for this model of a mountain landscape is shown on the next page. To make it you will need a few supplies. Contour models are often made of cardboard, cut out with a special kind of knife called an X-Acto knife. However, this is a difficult and risky process, since X-Acto knives are extremely sharp and hard to handle. Unless one of your parents, or another adult, wants to help you with this project, I suggest using other tools and materials.

It is possible to cut cardboard (like the kind boxes are made of) with ordinary scissors. However, this can be frustrating and difficult, especially if there is a lot of cutting to do, so I will mention another alternative: Styrofoam. The problem with Styrofoam is that you can't find it for free in a closet or in the basement, but the good thing about it is that it's very easy to cut. Most art supply shops or craft stores sell thin sheets of Styrofoam about one quarter of an inch thick.

Whether you decide to use Styrofoam or cardboard for this model, the material needs to be between an eighth and a quarter of an inch thick (the thicker the better). Before you start cutting, you will need to trace each contour line on the pattern onto a separate piece of paper. Put a piece of fairly thin paper over the pattern, and trace the biggest contour line onto it. This line on the pattern is identified with a number 1, so after you trace it onto your paper, put a number 1 in the middle of it.

Now trace the next biggest contour line (line number 2) onto a different sheet of paper, and put a number 2 in the middle of it. Continue this process until every contour line on the pattern has been transferred onto a separate sheet of paper and identified with the correct number. When you get to the smaller contour lines, several of them will fit on one piece of paper.

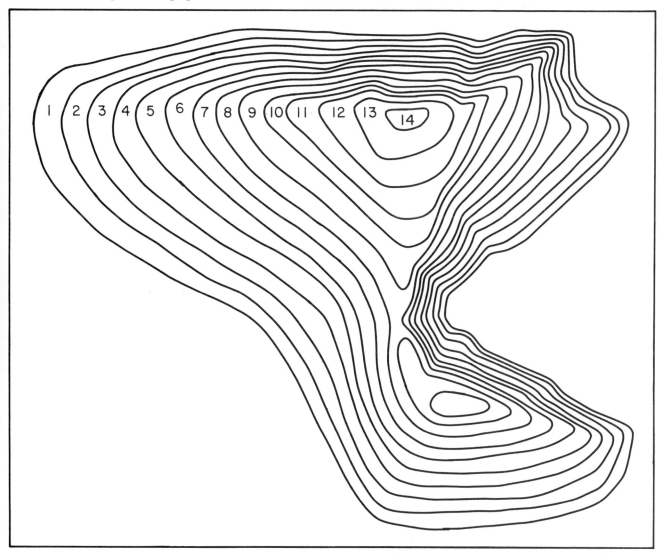

Next, glue each piece of paper onto a sheet of cardboard or Styrofoam that has been cut to approximately the right size, and cut around the contour line. You will end up with a pile of jellyfish-like shapes that now need to be put together into the form of mountains. Look back at the pattern on page 67. Notice how on one side of the mountains the contour lines are much closer together than on the other side. As you glue the layers of the model together, try to line them up just as they are on the pattern. When you have put all the layers together, you will have a three-dimensional model that shows you exactly how contour lines work.

——— Map-Reading Exercise ———

For this exercise, you will use the topo map on page 64, which is part of a wilderness area.

1. What signs do you see that humans have used and changed the landscape?

2. If you hiked over the top of Arapaho Pass, what would your highest elevation be?

3. If you wanted to go eat your lunch by Caribou Lake, which way would you turn at the top of the pass?

4. Which way would you turn at the top of the pass if you wanted a less-steep descent?

5. Which trail on the north side of Arapaho Pass is the first to cross a creek? How many times does it cross it?

6. You are planning a two-day backpacking trip and have gotten a wilderness permit from the local authorities to spend one night in the wilderness area. You are starting from and returning the next day to a *trailhead* that is just off the bottom of the map — the beginning of the Arapaho Pass trail. You don't want to hike more than four or five miles into your chosen camp, and you want to camp below tree line (which is around eleven thousand feet) and near a stream. It would be best to camp fairly near a trail, and on level or gently sloping terrain. Look at the trails on the map and design your route. Use the bar scale beneath the map to estimate distances. Decide where you would like to camp, and plan a short hike for the morning of the second day, before you head back to the trailhead.

Answers: 1. Trails, roads, and mines. 2. 11,906 feet. 3. Right. 4. Left. 5. The trail to the right; it crosses the creek three times.

7

Wayfinding in the City

Most of us, when we think of wayfinding, imagine a journey through some sort of wilderness. And even though we know that wayfinding is a skill that is used to get from any one place to any other, so far we've concentrated on country or wilderness areas. We've talked about wayfinding in the featureless environments of the ocean, the Arctic, and the desert. We've talked about celestial navigation and pilotage, and about orienteering in the hills and the mountains. But one environment we haven't considered yet is the city.

Imagine the information-gathering machine we talked about in Chapter 3. Picture it as a stocky little robot, standing on the corner of the busiest street in Mexico City, receiving information from all its monitoring devices. People are rushing by it in every direction, pushing and pulling, laughing and arguing. Some of them are crying out to the crowd to buy their gum, pencils, shoe shines, and tomatoes. The entire street is rumbling and shaking from the passing of a huge, ancient, diesel truck, full of confused and complaining cows.

On another corner a blind man with a beautiful voice is singing Mexican love songs. Behind him, a street vendor hollers over the noise of his steam-operated quesadilla machine, advertising his delicious wares as the machine erupts from time to time with an ear-splitting shriek and the smell of burning cheese.

When the streetlight turns red, a young man in the middle of the intersection walks from vehicle to vehicle with a burning torch in his hand, swallowing the flames and then shooting them back out of his mouth. In the other direction, cars, buses, trucks, bikes, motorcycles, and even an occasional ox cart, are whizzing and wheezing by, honking horns, and belching exhaust fumes.

In short, this particular street corner is a continuous explosion of sights, sounds, smells, tastes, and sensations. Our small machine, made to gather and process information, is emitting strange little bleeps. It moves a few feet in one direction, returns to its spot, and then moves a few feet in another. Finally it starts spinning in place, springs springing, lights blinking, and steam coming out of its aural receptors. "Help, help," it bleeps, "get me out of here!"

Have you ever felt that way? Just about anyone who visits a busy city for the first time has. There is more information than the brain can process, so it just shuts some of the sensations out. This is called information overload, and almost everyone has experienced it at one time or another. It is one reason why wayfinding in the city can be so difficult.

How can you avoid information overload? Cities are so rich in messages for your senses that you have to learn which of those messages to pay attention to. Your brain shuts down because it doesn't know which signals, of the thousands it is receiving, it can ignore. You have to know beforehand what information you need. In other words, you need to know where you are going and how to get there, or how to find out how to get there if you don't already know. Once you know where you are going in a city, you can enjoy the thousands of sensations that are constantly bombarding you.

You might imagine that one problem with wayfinding in the city is that all of the messages your senses send to your brain are interesting, but only some of them are useful. Your eyes don't *want* to ignore the sight of the young man swallowing fire . . . they're glued to him as he walks back and forth among the cars. Your nose and your tongue are pulling you toward the quesadilla man, and your ears want to hear more of the beautiful Mexican love songs. Can you pay attention to all these things and still get where you are going? Yes, but if you are wayfinding you have to learn to concentrate on certain things. As we know, each of our senses can bring us important wayfinding information. All we have to do is learn what to notice.

How about our eyes? What kinds of wayfinding messages are there in the city for our eyes? The most obvious ones are landmarks, and the most obvious of these are street signs. On almost every street corner in almost every big city in the world, there are signs that identify the streets that intersect there.

Remember that streets are lines of position for navigating a city. If you know where you want to go, you can plan your route beforehand (probably using a street map) and know exactly what streets to look for and where to turn. Using street signs for landmarks is the first step, but if you're in a city for a few days you'll notice that your brain picks and chooses its own landmarks, most of them more interesting than street signs. Instead of looking for the sign that says 16th and Broadway, for instance, you'll notice that there's an ice cream store on that corner, and you'll always know where you are when you see that store.

What about when you're just exploring a city — not going anyplace in particular, but just walking around looking at things? In that situation, even though you aren't looking for any particular location, you *do* have to get back to your starting point (your hotel, a friend's house, or wherever you are staying). First of all, when you visit a new city, try to find out how the streets are laid out. Many modern cities are laid out so that the streets run north-south and east-west, making a square grid.

Even when cities are not laid out on a square grid (and most very old cities in the world aren't), it is always helpful to know which direction is which. There are many indications of direction in the city, just as there are in the country. Some of them are made by people, and some are natural.

Just as in the country, there are prevailing winds in the city. If you learn the direction of the prevailing wind, you will be able to recognize many of the same signs you would see in the country. A combination of wind and sun causes paint to fade and peel, and you can often observe that one side of a building, fence, or bridge has a more "weathered" appearance than the other. In the Northern Hemisphere, the north side of a building generally gets more shade than the south, east, or west sides, so you will find more moss, lichen, ivy, and other shade-loving plants growing on the north side. In the winter, snow lingers much longer on the north side of a building than the other sides.

Our sense of touch is very active in the city. For one thing, we feel the vibration of the ground under our feet, both from heavy vehicles passing over the surface and from rapid transit cars traveling underground. The rumbling of the sidewalk can help us identify where we

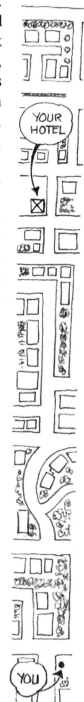

are. Our sense of touch also gives us directional information. The "sun walk" and "wind walk" have city variations: in the winter when it is cold, people want to walk on the sunny side of the street; in the summer, everyone crosses over to the shady side. Walking against a prevailing wind, especially when it's cold, can be very uncomfortable, but it does give us a clue about directions.

Our hearing also brings us lots of wayfinding information in the city. In San Francisco, the ringing of the cable-car bells identifies certain streets. In New York City, the sound of boat horns tells us we are close to the water. Certain streets and intersections have very distinctive sounds. There might be a music store somewhere that plays music over loudspeakers, or a street with lots of vendors selling their wares. Our ears can learn to identify certain locations with certain sounds, and we can know where we are by what we hear.

There is probably more information for our noses in the city than in the country. It is possible to recognize entire districts by the way they smell. Places like Fisherman's Wharf, Chinatown, and Little Italy can be recognized by the wonderful smells they create. Large bakeries leak delicious aromas into the air along with steam and heat from their ovens. You can often smell a harbor before you can see it. Certain factories also produce very distinct odors — usually not as pleasant as those from bakeries, but just as recognizable.

When you visit a new city, learn to notice all these things. Use the information that your senses collect. Pay attention to your environment and learn to use its messages. Practice wayfinding in the city as carefully as if you were backpacking in the mountains.

In the first chapter we talked about the difference between public ways and private ways. Private ways, whether you are in the country or the city, are your own personal routes from one place to another, and private waysigns are things that your own brain has picked out to help identify certain paths and locations. In the city there are many large landmarks that serve this purpose. Tall buildings make great private landmarks. If you can find a particular landmark, like a tall building, tower, or hill, you can use it the same way you use a high mountain in the wilderness. Keep track of your position relative to that landmark, and no matter which way you turn, remember where you have started and where you are going in relation to your landmark.

Here's an example of a girl who used the landmark technique for wayfinding in the city. When Sally was twelve, she won a violin competition in her own small town in the United States and was sent to Vienna, Austria, to compete. She hadn't had much experience in cities and was almost as nervous about being in a foreign city as she was about playing her violin for some of the best musicians in Europe. When she arrived in Vienna she was given an information packet that included a map of the city. She studied the map in her hotel room and hoped she'd get the chance to do some exploring on her own.

There were many other English-speaking students there, and one day they all met for lunch near Saint Stephen's Cathedral. They had the afternoon free, and Sally and several of the other children decided to explore the area. They were told to meet back with the rest of the group at three o'clock, at an outside café near the east side of the cathedral. You can see on the map on the next page that Saint Stephen's is just about in the middle of the old section of Vienna.

Several of the children wanted to see the antique musical instruments in the museum at the Imperial Palace, but Sally was the only one who had her map with her and could figure out how to get there. (Her map was actually much more complicated than the one in this book because it had all the street names on it.)

Sally got the group to the museum with no problem, and on the way back she decided to try an experiment. She wanted to walk through some of the beautiful old winding streets, and she wanted to do it without the map. The tall spire of Saint Stephen's was visible from just about anyplace in the city, so she decided to orient herself by using the cathedral to constantly keep track of her position. As the group wandered through the old city, Sally kept the location of the cathedral fixed in her mind even when she couldn't see it.

After a few hours, they had gone far enough that they were on the opposite side of the cathedral from where they had started, but Sally knew exactly where they were and was able to guide them to the café, where they met the rest of the group. Most of the other children hadn't been paying attention to where they were going, and some of them were amazed when Sally led them back to the café. She knew that she didn't have any kind of special ability, but that by concentrating, paying

VIENNA

••• Orienting by map

······· Orienting by cathedral

attention, and thinking about what she was doing, she was able to find her way in a big and confusing city.

Many cities have good public transportation systems, and in some cities you can get almost anywhere by using the rapid transit. To use the rapid transit method of wayfinding, just get a city map and a rapid transit map, and learn the city according to the subway stops. You need a map of the city to find out where you are and where you want to go, and a map of the transit system to figure out how to do it. Carry both maps with you at all times.

In other cities public transportation is more of a problem, and you might find yourself in some unusual situations as you try to get around. In Calcutta, India, where Vic went for the ice cream cone, one of the most common forms of transportation is the bicycle rickshaw. In southern Mexico, people jump helter-skelter into the backs of Volkswagen vans and just holler when they want to get off. No matter what the transportation system is, it is important to understand how to use it.

Wayfinding in the city can be fascinating and fun. Here are some city activities to help you learn how.

Scavenger Hunt

For this game you will need three things: a map of the city you're in, a person to go exploring with, and permission from your parents to go exploring. Here is what you will do: you and your partner will each choose the other's journey, using the city map as a guide. Decide on a destination for the other person, and mark a route to it on the map. Then you will make the journeys.

Your partner will go with you on your journey, but you must do the wayfinding according to the route marked on the map (then you'll accompany your partner as he or she follows the route you've marked). You will each collect and bring back five objects that will prove you've been on the journey. Here are some examples of things to bring back, and places to get them: matchbooks (from hotels and restaurants), deposit slips or other blank forms (from banks), sales receipts (from any store where you buy something, no matter how little it costs), business stamps on a blank piece of paper.

Some of these items are available to any quiet and polite person who walks in and takes them, and others can only be gotten from a person behind a counter. If you politely explain, for instance, that you would like a book of matches, most restaurant or hotel employees will be glad to give you one. Most business establishments have a rubber stamp with the name of the business on it, and if you hand the clerk a blank piece of paper, he or she will probably stamp it for you. After you have successfully completed your journey, you will have five souvenirs of the city.

City Walk

This activity is designed to sharpen your nonvisual senses. In it you will be walking blind with your partner (or leading your blind partner). Obviously, the person who's leading needs to know where she or he is going, and that might mean advance planning with the city map. If you are being led, simply close your eyes, and hold your partner's arm as you take the walk. Your partner will tell you exactly when to step up or down, when to stop and go, and give you any other verbal cues you will need.

You must relax as much as possible, trust your partner (you can see that the partner's job is serious), and pay attention to all your senses. Listen to the traffic. How many streets did you cross? What other noises did you hear? Pay attention to what you are smelling and try to identify odors. Make guesses about where you are. See if you can feel the vibrations in the streets and sidewalks from vehicles passing on or below the surface.

When you return from your walk, write down everything you can remember in your journal: smells, sounds, sensations, and — if you eat anything (hot pretzels, nuts, popcorn) — tastes. Make a guess about where you've been, and then take the same walk with your eyes open. Were the two journeys similar? Now it is your partner's turn.

8

What If You Do Get Lost?

Before we finish, there's one more thing I'd like to talk about. I would like to leave you with some suggestions about what to do if you should ever lose your way. We will talk about two kinds of being lost: lost in the country, and lost in the city.

First of all, the most important thing to know about being lost is that you have to keep your mind clear for thinking. In other words, *don't panic*. Even if it's a scary situation, give yourself a few minutes to calm down before you make any big moves. If you are lost in the wilderness, remember that there are people close by who are at least as anxious to find you as you are to be found, and if everyone thinks clearly and without panic, that's just what will happen. If you are lost in the city, there will be people around that you can ask for help.

When you are hiking or backpacking, there are certain things you should always carry with you. The trouble is, one of the times when people get lost in the wilderness is when they think they are going only a "short" distance away from camp (to get water, dig a latrine, or just be alone for a few minutes), and so they don't have their packs with them. Even though they might have emergency and first-aid provisions, their packs are left leaning up against a tree back at camp.

Since that is often the case, there are some things that you should always carry somewhere on your body. The most important of these is a good, loud whistle. Get one that makes lots of noise, and hang it around your neck. Remember that it is an emergency signaling device and should *never* be used except in the case of a real emergency. If you get lost or separated from the rest of your group, or if you are hurt and can't catch up with them, you can create a loud signal that can be heard for quite a distance.

The international distress signal is a series of three repeated signals of any kind. So blow three blasts on your whistle, pause for a little while, blow three more blasts, pause, and keep repeating the signal. Once you are certain that you are lost or in need of help, stay where you are. Don't continue wandering around, because the chances are that you will wander in the wrong direction and get even further separated from your group.

Some of the other things you should always carry with you are: water (you can get the kind of bottle that hangs from your belt) and water purifying tablets, a pocket knife, matches in a plastic Baggie, and some sort of high-energy food (trail mix, a high-protein candy bar, or anything else you can think of that will fit in your pockets). These are things you can keep with you at all times, even when you don't have your pack. Another suggestion, though it may sound pretty strange, is to carry a large plastic trash bag in one of your pockets. Plastic is good insulation, besides being waterproof, and if you cut a slit in the top and two in the sides for your head and arms, you will have a ready-made body warmer.

If you become lost in the wilderness, stay calm, try to keep warm, avoid fatigue, and try to find a way of signaling your location. If you are lost for more than a few hours and find yourself in a survival sit-

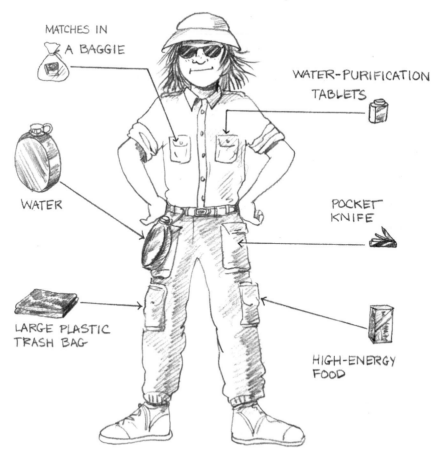

MATCHES IN A BAGGIE

WATER-PURIFICATION TABLETS

WATER

POCKET KNIFE

LARGE PLASTIC TRASH BAG

HIGH-ENERGY FOOD

uation, establish a camp. The best place for this is high, clear ground, but it is better to stay where you are than to wander for miles looking for a good location. If you need to leave your camp (to look for firewood or water, for instance), mark a clear trail so you can find your way back. Don't ever try to travel at night.

When you are lost, you want to improve the situation without further endangering yourself. The last thing you want to do is make things worse, so think before you do anything. If you decide to climb a tree to get a better view, for example, choose a safe one that is easy to get up and down.

Because fires are visible for great distances, especially at night, it is possible to use them as emergency signals. Airplanes flying overhead, or any other searchers, may take note of your fire and report it or come to investigate. But fires can also be terribly dangerous. If you decide to build a fire, do it right. Choose a clear place well away from trees with low-hanging branches. Make a stone ring and dig a shallow pit in the center of it. Before you build the fire, gather as much firewood as you can and keep it well away from the blaze. You can keep the fire small by feeding it only small amounts of wood. Watch over it constantly. DO NOT LET A FIRE GET OUT OF CONTROL, AND NEVER BUILD A FIRE IN STRONG WIND.

Few of us have ever seen a raging forest fire, but anyone who has knows what it can do. You need to respect fire and have a good, healthy terror of it getting out of control. If you get lost, the chances are that you will survive; if you are in a forest fire, the chances are that you won't. It is that simple, so be careful with fire. When you are camping with your family or any other group, ask someone to teach you how to make and maintain a safe fire.

Being lost in the city involves a completely different set of problems. If you are lost in a city where people speak English, at least you can ask for help. But even in that case, you have to know what to ask. No matter where you are, if you are visiting a strange city, be sure to carry something with you that has your address on it. This can be especially important in countries where people don't speak English.

If you are staying in a hotel, carry a piece of hotel stationery or a book of matches that identifies the hotel and its location. Have someone write, in the language that is spoken there, something like "Please take me to" or "Where is" next to the address. Talk to your parents or the group you are traveling with, and establish a rule that if anyone gets separated, they will meet the rest of the group back at the hotel. This will save wear and tear on everyone's nerves.

It is easier to get lost in a city than you might think. I was once walking in New Delhi, India, with an American family. We were making our way down an extremely crowded street when their little girl very suddenly just disappeared. One minute she was there, and the next she was lost in the crowd. There were thousands of people on the sidewalk,

and she disappeared into the masses. Fortunately, we soon found her again, but we had a frightening few moments when we thought about how impossible it would be to find anyone in that crowd of people whose language we didn't speak.

If you are lost in the city, the best person to ask for help, whether you speak the language or not, is a policeman. Don't be afraid to ask; it is his job to give assistance. If you can't find a uniformed policeman, go into any fairly prosperous-looking business establishment and ask one of the employees to help you. People will most likely be very interested and sympathetic, and if you are a shy person you might not like all the attention, but someone will see that you get back to the address you have written on the piece of paper.

Whether you are lost in the city or the wilderness, keep a clear head and make thoughtful decisions. Don't panic. Someone is looking for you, too, and if you're careful and smart you'll find each other. The best way to avoid the problem of needing to get found, of course, is not to get lost. Practice wayfinding as if your life depends on it, and enjoy the journeys that take you on your way.

Index